ANCIENT W)

HISTORY, INDUSTRY AND CRAFTS

Ian D. Rotherham

SHIRE PUBLICATIONS

Published in Great Britain in 2014 by Shire Publications Ltd,
PO Box 883, Oxford OX1 9PL, United Kingdom.
PO Box 3985, New York, NY 10185-3983, USA.
E-mail: shire@shirebooks.co.uk · www.shirebooks.co.uk

A CIP catalogue record for this book is available from the
British Library.

Shire Library no. 697 · ISBN-13: 978 0 74781 165 7

Ian D. Rotherham has asserted his right under the
Copyright, Designs and Patents Act, 1988, to be identified
as the author of this book.

Designed by Tony Truscott Designs, Sussex, UK
Typeset in Perpetua and Gill Sans.
Printed in China through World Print Ltd.

14 15 16 17 18   11 10 9 8 7 6 5 4 3 2

COVER IMAGE
Cover design by Peter Ashley. Front cover: Spray of oak
leaves in woodland on the Sandringham Estate, Norfolk,
photograph by Peter Ashley. Back cover detail: Farm
wagon by S.R. Badmin from the Puffin Picture Book
Trees in Britain.

TITLE PAGE IMAGE
Clog-block makers in the woods were a common sight
from the eighteenth century onwards. Beech or sycamore
were preferred for their hardness but many clogs were
made from alder. (A clog-maker in North Wales assures
me that alder was chosen because it was soft and easy to
work, but that it produced poor-quality clogs.)

CONTENTS PAGE IMAGE
Old Oaks on Wickham Common in Kent, after a painting
by S. Johnson and published as a postcard by Raphael Tuck
& Sons (oilette, 1920s to 1930s). The typical ancient
pollard oaks of a 'working' common are shown.

ACKNOWLEDGEMENTS
I wish to thank all those who over many years have
contributed to the studies, the events and the enthusiasm
connected with ancient woods and old trees. Donald
Pigott at Lancaster University unknowingly kick-started
my passion for woods and trees back in the 1970s. Paul
Ardron, Christine Handley, Mel Jones, Ted Green, Oliver
Gilbert, Barry Wright, Paul Smith and many others have
all helped along the way. Mauro Agnoletti and various
international colleagues have helped provide international
context. They are all thanked for their generous help,
guidance, interest, and above all, patience. The series
editors at Shire Books are thanked for their work on
the final product.

IMAGE ACKNOWLEDGEMENTS
Paul Ardron, pages 19 and 29 (top). All other images are
from the author's collection.

CONTENTS

INTRODUCTION

Cᴏɴᴛʀᴀʀʏ ᴛᴏ ᴘᴏᴘᴜʟᴀʀ ʙᴇʟɪᴇꜰ, Britain's ancient woodlands are not 'wildwoods', or even remnants of 'wildwood'. These truly cultural landscapes mix nature and human history, woven as uniquely rich tapestries of ecology and history. The story of the woods is there to be 'read' if you have time, enthusiasm, and this book, which will take you from prehistory

Ancient hazel coppice, Lathkill Dale, Derbyshire.

to the present day. The types of landscape, geology and climate, and even differences in industries and manufacturing history, have placed varying demands on woods to create strong regional distinctiveness. This has led to woods developing local character depending on the ecological type of woodland present originally, and then the varying uses to which it has been put over the centuries by craftsmen as diverse as the bodgers of the Chilterns and the tan-bark merchants of Cumbria.

There is widespread popular and academic interest in woodlands and their history and archaeology. Yet there is little literature that addresses these topics. Based on over twenty years of field and archival research, this book is unique in bringing together this information in a single accessible volume. With the publication in 2008 of the *Woodland Heritage Manual* there is now

Ancient small-leaved lime, Whitwell Wood.

an accepted approach to the subject and interest in this long-neglected field is growing rapidly. The subject covers a wide range of topics, from extractive industries in woods, to the crafts based on extraction or harvesting of woodland products, and their processing. For centuries, these crafts were at the centre of British society, fundamental in the creation and protection of many of the landscapes we value today. However, as technologies changed and markets for products evolved, many of the woodland traditions and crafts were abandoned and forgotten, with just a few of the old crafts surviving to the present day. The footprints of lost craftsmen are indelibly etched into every ancient wood across the country; the only problem is in recognising and understanding the evidence. Even the wild woodland flowers and their distribution reflects the one-time uses of the sites, as do the formerly 'worked' trees. Humps and bumps of soil are now archaeology. These woods contain uniquely rich diversities of features ancient and modern, from wood banks and ditches, to trackways, charcoal hearths, Q-pits, bell-pits, quarries and building platforms.

Reading these landscapes can take you back over four thousand years of history, even in urban ancient woodland. It can help us reconstruct the local landscape and its unique history. Not only is the evidence physically imprinted into the environment, but woods and wooded landscapes are also recorded in place names, settlement names, and field names such as Wood End, Wood Lane, Hagg Side, Hollins End, Endowood, Woodseats, Woodthorpe, Willowgarth, Owlerton and the like. Woodseats, for example, would be 'the cottages deep in the wood', and Clayroyd a 'woodland clearing with clayey soil'. From early

Wood and timber were of great importance before plastic was invented. Here is a bread oven door from the 1600s, carved from oak.

The most familiar woodland flower and often an indicator of an old woodland site – the native bluebell.

medieval times, woods were themselves named: Park Spring or Parkwood Springs (the park coppice wood), West Haigh Wood (the enclosed wood), Newfield Spring (the coppice wood by the new field), and many others. Family names also reflect the wooded past with Underwood, Woodward, Hurst, Frith, Wood, Turner, Collier, Greenwood, Tanner, Forester, Warren, Warrender, Stubbs and Parker being just a few examples.

To walk through an ancient wood is to tread in the footsteps of the ghosts of those who once lived and worked in the medieval and early industrial countryside. The ancient wood is frequently part of a greater landscape of medieval park, of common or heath, of chase or forest. This book helps unravel the mysteries of the past now locked away in soils and trees. Identifying ancient coppice stools, stubbed boundary trees, or veteran pollards from a long-forgotten deer park or old hedgerow will bring an understanding of how the countryside looked and functioned in times past. These wonderful ancient landscapes come to life as the history of woodland workers and others over a thousand years or more is unfurled.

In many cases, there are strong regional differences and identities that persist in the woods of today. These may relate to particular industries and intensive uses, such as the Derbyshire and south Yorkshire charcoal makers who worked so hard to fuel the Industrial Revolution. With practice, these regional identities can be recognised and identified. Fragments of ancient woods are to be discovered as broad 'hedgerows' along old sunken lanes and trackways in urban and countryside areas, often still with veteran trees and woodland indicator plants. They are found close to rivers and streams, in green spaces such as golf courses, and even on modern housing estates – it is just a matter of looking.

Finally, the study of woods and woodlands lends itself to the local group and the local enthusiast, and almost everyone will have one or more suitable sites that are accessible. Many woods remain hardly known and little understood. Studying the local area can make a real and lasting contribution to knowledge and understanding of these most iconic and important, but often misunderstood, landscapes. Step inside a local wood and, with practice, one can read its landscape and its ecology like the pages of a book. Ancient woodlands are remarkable repositories of the history and archaeology of the woodland and its management; also of the people and communities who have lived in that landscape, perhaps as long ago as prehistoric times. Oddly, they have until recently been largely overlooked by archaeologists. This is not always the case when there is obvious major heritage on a site, such as some of the Chiltern beech woods. Here the massive prehistoric fortifications are well documented. Yet in the heart of the city of Sheffield, in Ecclesall Woods, an entire hilltop enclosure, a Romano-British field system, a medieval deer-park boundary, and hundreds of charcoal hearths, lay undiscovered until about ten years ago.

Timber and small wood were vital for most buildings. A magnificent timber house in Sundridge, Kent.

More recently, two other more modern forms of woodland archaeology have come to light. These are the extensive but sometimes enigmatic remains of wartime and military use of the woods, from bomb craters to trenches and gun positions. These date from the Napoleonic wars to the Cold War military activities of the 1950s and 1960s. The second type is what Paul Ardron and I have described as 'community archaeology': the dens and play areas of children and young people. These include BMX tracks and for example, the rough shelters sometimes built for war-gaming or by itinerants. All these activities are adding to the centuries-old palimpsest of the woods.

The Charcoal Burner – a postcard souvenir from the Royal Lancashire Show, Village Industries.

WHAT IS AN 'ANCIENT' WOOD?

WHAT MAKES a wood 'ancient' and why are Britain's ancient woods so special? How did woods evolve and how do they link to the past? Why were they protected and what does that mean for wooded landscapes today? In Britain, landscapes with ancient trees occur in two main settings: 'wood pasture' and 'coppice'. Sometimes, these two land-uses vary through time and are overlaid, so the modern wood may have evidence of both. This is one of the fascinations of woodland detective work; if trees have survived from centuries past, then they surely tell a story of woodland origins and management traditions.

THE WOOD PASTURE TRADITION

Wood pasture, the *silva pastilis* of the Domesday Book, occurred in three forms: royal forests and their private equivalent, 'chases'; wooded commons; and deer parks. Royal forests and the private forests of the aristocracy flourished after the Norman Conquest of 1066. In this context, the word 'forest' does not necessarily mean or imply woodland. 'Forest' here is a legal term for land on which 'Forest Law' applied, relating to hunting of deer, grazing of animals, clearing of land and felling of timber. Forests and chases were not fenced and could include within their boundaries woodland, heath, moorland, fen, farmland and settlements. Wooded commons, forests and chases could contain large numbers of veteran trees, and included 'woods' individually named and carefully demarcated.

In the sixteenth and seventeenth centuries, many well-wooded deer parks were converted into compartmented coppice woods or 'improved' for agriculture. Some were modified and incorporated into great eighteenth- and nineteenth-century grand estates with extensively planted woodlands as a setting for a great house.

Although there are records of parks without trees, deer parks usually consisted of large, open-grown trees (mostly oak), some woodlands protected from grazing, and areas largely cleared of trees (with grass or heath). The park livestock could graze in the open and find cover in unenclosed wooded areas.

Opposite:
The Big Oak at Pontfadog in Wales is one of the oldest oaks in Britain and is shown here on a postcard from the early twentieth century. Its history and mythology are celebrated: 'In Pontfadog lives the oldest oak tree in Britain which was spared when King Henry II had his men cut down the Ceiriog Woods in 1165.'

The cleared areas called 'launds' (often called 'lawns' on maps today), or 'plains', had grassland or heath with scattered big trees. Many trees in the launds would have been pollarded – that is, cut at least 6 feet from the ground leaving a massive lower trunk called a 'bolling' above which, a continuous crop of new growth sprouts, out of reach of the grazing deer, sheep and cattle. In the launds, regeneration of trees was restricted because of continual grazing and new trees were only able to grow in the protection of thickets of hawthorn, blackthorn and holly. Some of the un-pollarded timber trees reached a great age and size and were sought-after for major building projects.

Wooded commons were unfenced areas where commoners had rights to graze animals and to take products such as fuel and building materials. These commoners were persons holding land in the open fields, or tenants of the manorial lord with certain rights on the manor's common land. Their rights were strictly regulated and administered; this was not a free-for-all. Commoners could usually cut underwood, harvest wood from pollards, and take dead wood, but not fell timber trees. These common rights were called 'estovers' or 'botes' (for example, hedgebote wood for making fences; housebote for housebuilding and cartbote for making farm vehicles).

THE COPPICE TRADITION

From the Middle Ages until the second part of the nineteenth century, ancient woods throughout the country were managed as coppices (*silva minuta*), either

A 1930s example of a particular use of coppice wood with on-site manufacture – stacked tent pegs for the army from an oak and beech wood.

as simple coppice or as 'coppice-with-standards'. In coppice woods, the trees were periodically (generally every ten to thirty years, but as often as once a year) cut down to the ground to what is called a 'stool'; from the stool grew multiple stems, called coppice or 'underwood'. The poles of wood were said to 'spring' from the stool, hence the names of many coppice woods include the word 'spring'. Indeed, in many areas local people think a 'spring-wood' name is to do with the season or water; it is not, and it provides sure evidence of antiquity. In a coppice-

A charcoal burner's hut in Old Park Wood, Sheffield, early 1900s, showing the traditional and primitive wigwam structure.

with-standards, some trees were not coppiced but allowed to grow on to become mature single-stemmed trees. These were the standards, and were of various ages. The coppice provided 'wood' and the standard trees provided 'timber'. The timber trees, mainly oak, were for building projects, but their by-products of bark and 'lop and top', were also of economic value. Coppice was used for making hurdles, for house building, for tools, and for ancient trackways such as those crossing prehistoric fenlands. One of the oldest, best-recorded and most important uses of coppice poles was for charcoal making, but a vast number of other crafts and industries also depended on it. Coppice wood was essential for domestic purposes as it provided firewood used for heating and cooking. Before the introduction of sweet chestnut coppice, ash, hornbeam and alder poles were used extensively in the hop industry in the south-east of England and in Herefordshire. These formed the frameworks up which the hop-bines could be trained.

Coppice woods were valuable and particularly vulnerable to grazing damage in the first few years after cutting. For this reason, they were surrounded by stock-proof barriers: fences, banks with external ditches, stone walls, hedges, or a combination. Where woodland boundary features survive, they provide archaeological evidence, telling a great deal about the wood, its extent, and its management. The woods had also to be protected against human thieves and trespassers. This was particularly important in autumn when berries and fruits were ripe, and in winter when firewood supplies were low.

Coppice woods often originated in park or forests areas and sometimes replaced them when wood pasture was enclosed for wood production. Many 'wooded' or ancient 'treed' landscapes exist today but are largely overlooked or misidentified. The ghosts, shadows, or footprints of anciently wooded areas still survive, so-metimes intact, and sometimes with barely a trace left.

WHY ARE ANCIENT WOODS SPECIAL?

The Major Oak in Sherwood Forest, is an ancient, open-grown forest oak rather than a pollard. Through the Robin Hood myths and Hollywood, this is probably the most famous tree in the world.

Technically, to qualify as 'ancient' a woodland has to be proved to have existed as a 'wood' as long ago as either 1700 or 1600, depending on which of the two authorities – George Peterken and Oliver Rackham, respectively – you are referring to. The logic behind these dates is that there was little active planting of woodland in Britain before this time. So if a wood is as old as this, it is likely to be very old and probably 'semi-natural' in origin, in which case the woodland will have distinctive animals and plants mostly found only in wooded environments. These species often demand particular environmental conditions that are met in a wood, but often lost outside it, particularly

Yet each has a unique story to tell in its own quiet history. Commons, heaths, fens, roadside verges, hedgerows, urban parks, and even gardens: all may have evidence of Britain's woodland past. For the landscape detective this is a truly exciting prospect.

FINDING AND SURVEYING AN ANCIENT WOOD

The first step in finding an ancient wood is to look at a map; begin with a modern-day Ordnance Survey map, preferably at 1:25,000 scale. This should show place-names, field boundaries, lanes and trackways, and of course, the woods themselves. Then look online at Google Earth or a similar website that provides decent aerial photographs of the area. Now you may be ready to undertake your first reconnoitre; armed with a map and a notepad you need little else for a first foray into the unknown. At this early stage, the intention is simply to cover the ground and seek evidence of woodland.

in the drier eastern and south-eastern parts of Britain, where the environment beyond the woodland is often totally inhospitable to these special plants and animals. Another factor is that, once beyond the woodland boundary, human management of the land is different; frequently it is this which has removed our special fauna and flora.

If woodland is ancient, then to a greater or lesser extent, it will have the unique ecology of a woodland 'habitat', and the remarkable record of human life and work within the wood. The human imprint is preserved through time as what historians describe as a 'palimpsest' or multi-layered landscape. Because the woodland has largely been protected from the worst excesses of modern machinery and gross disturbance of the terrain, then the lesser footprint of former populations on soil, ecology, and landscape is still there to be discovered. This is the unique importance of ancient wooded landscapes and is why so many people get excited to find one on their doorstep. Remarkably, for such a rich and precious

Yellow archangel – one of the best indicator species to be found within ancient woodland.

environmental resource, they are still to be found in most parts of Britain. Many have been lost, particularly in the last fifty or sixty years, and innumerable sites are damaged beyond repair. However, part of their importance is as a rich and diverse resource of heritage and archaeology alongside their rich ecology, accessible to everyone.

A clear idea of the terrain can be identified from maps and aerial photography – this could be a modern wooded landscape or one with few trees remaining. In the absence of an obviously ancient wood today, place-names, field-names, and lane-names may indicate where one used to be. The map work will pay dividends as the search begins.

Alongside the clues and evidence already described, there are other things to look for and places to search to drill down for detail. The parish boundary is often a good starting point since our ancient coppice woods were often formed from the wooded landscapes that remained at the periphery of a settlement as the human population grew and put pressure on the environmental resource. The earlier countryside up to around the time of the Norman Conquest was dominated by grazed wooded areas called wood-pastures, but as the population increased up to the fifteenth century, 'woods' had to be protected. Now managed as 'coppice', these were enclosed

Coppice woodland produce – wattle hurdles or fences stacked to dry out in the 1930s.

by ditches, hedges, walls and other boundaries such as fences, to keep people and livestock out and to allow the young trees and 'sprouts' of coppice, to 'spring' up. The 'cut and come again' system of coppicing to produce 'wood' or 'underwood', together with the longer cycle of using timber from the bigger trees in the woodland canopy, was rigorously planned and implemented by specialist woodland craftsmen, often over many centuries. One of the most damaging things for a young coppice wood was grazing by animals, especially domestic livestock; hence the need for a secure boundary. Animals would often be let in at a later date once the coppice had grown sufficiently to be out of harm's way.

It is good to walk around the wood as well as through it. Look to see whether today's boundaries match those of earlier times; has the wood either expanded or, more likely, contracted? What sort of boundaries are they, and are they old or new? Paths, trackways, bridleways and lanes through the wood are also of great interest. These may link the site to other places in the parish, perhaps today or maybe historically. The patterns of routes are worth investigating, as they may simply be tracks to lead 'through' the wood, or they may have been used for taking produce 'out' of the wood; the implications are very different. If the track or lane has a name, then that too may be significant; these ancient routes form an important part of the archaeology.

WOODS, PARKS AND FORESTS

THE MEDIEVAL WOOD is just one of Britain's 'wooded landscapes', alongside parks, forests, commons and heaths; indeed, some medieval woods were within parks or forests. This chapter explores the relationships between parks, forests, woods, commons and heaths and introduces the people who lived and worked there.

In Britain, there are two broadly distinct 'ancient woodland' landscapes: coppice woods, with few obviously large trees, but strikingly rich and sometimes diverse ground floras (as described in the previous chapter); and parklands, which can link back to medieval parks. These areas generally have poorer ground floras due to grazing livestock, and are characterised by massive and ancient trees, chiefly pollards. In terms of wildlife conservation, it has been assumed that coppice woods provided an excellent habitat for woodland birds and flowers; parks were home to rare lichens and fungi growing on the trees, and insects or other invertebrates that depended on veteran tree dead-wood habitat.

Medieval parks were part of a suite of landscape types that mixed trees with grazing or browsing mammals. These included wood-pasture, wooded commons, and forests as relicts of a great wooded savannah across much of north-western Europe. Parks are 'pasture-woodland', related to forests, heaths, moors, and some commons, with grazing animals and variable tree cover. Aside from obvious external enclosures, they were essentially unenclosed grazing lands. In the two centuries following the Norman Conquest, the number of parks in England increased dramatically to perhaps three thousand or more, with possibly fifty

An obviously ancient oak tree – a closed woodland tree in Whitwell Wood, North Derbyshire, with a tall, straight trunk and high canopy.

in Wales, and eighty in Scotland. From the early thirteenth century, a royal licence was required to create a park in areas of royal forest, though in both England and Scotland baronial parks were created without licence. Where documents survive, they provide invaluable reference materials for a now vanished age, giving insight into landscape and ecology. The average English medieval park was around 100 acres, though size varied considerably.

Parks are different from the medieval coppice woods that sit alongside them and sometimes even within them; these enclosed landscapes are unique resources for conservation. They provide insights into ecological history, and research has transformed our understanding of the importance of parks for rare invertebrates. Until relatively recently, medieval parks were not considered to be 'ancient woodland' and were neglected by conservationists. Parks have trees (usually but not always), and large (and sometimes smaller) grazing mammals; in order to survive, trees need protection. Some parkland trees are ornamental and others are managed 'working' trees, with differences in species and form.

Parks share features with other unenclosed grazed landscapes with trees and woods: chases, forests, moors, heaths, commons and some fens.

Working the woods in the early 1900s. Note the heavy horses, the wagons, the harnesses and the chains.

THE ROAD THROUGH THE WOOD

These wooded and treed landscapes occurred almost everywhere and so too might their shadowy footprint today. Many parks 'took in' parts of earlier landscapes when they were enclosed from 'waste' or 'forest', and management may have allowed parts of this ancient ecology to survive. In other cases, parks include ecology and features from specific periods of active management (with specific ends and outcomes), from subsequent times of abandonment, or changed use. Each phase preserves, modifies, or removes earlier ecology, these working landscapes evolving over a thousand years or more.

The extensive medieval landscapes provided hunting, foodstuffs, and both timber and wood for building and fuel. As well as deer, medieval parks contained wild boar, hares, rabbits, game birds, fish in fishponds, and grazing for cattle and sheep. Pannage (feeding pigs on acorns from oaks) provided revenue in rents. Medieval parks had large areas of heath or grassland called 'launds', or plains dotted with trees. Parks had fallow deer (*Dama dama*), and red deer (*Cervus elaphus*) for the table and the hunt; this sometimes involved releasing the deer beyond the park pale into the chase beyond.

A massive medieval deer-park bank in north Derbyshire.

Large oaks were grown for timber; in some cases trunks and boughs were carefully nurtured to form particular shapes and sizes for specific functions. Careful planning and management over many decades are key aspects of park historical ecology. Most very old trees, often oak (*Quercus robur*), are specimens that were actively managed for several centuries and then abandoned. They range from youngsters of 400 years, to veterans of 800 to 1,200 years, and these trees were among the most precious resources of former medieval parks. Large trees provided shelter for cattle and deer in winter, shade in summer,

Woodlands became the terrain of gamekeepers and the haunts of poachers.

and herbage to feed livestock. Solitary trees in launds were 'pollarded' (high coppice) or shredded (branches removed from the tall, main stem). There were woods called holts or coppices, and special woods in some regions called 'hollings', 'hollins' or 'holly hags', where holly was cut on rotation to feed deer and other livestock in winter. For several months of the year – longer during colder periods – grass does not grow in Britain and livestock depended on stored hay and cut branches of evergreen holly. Pollarding extended the lifespan of trees and ensured a continuous supply of dead wood, a highly important wildlife habitat. The only new tree growth outside the woods was in protective thickets of hawthorn, holly, rose and bramble.

The park was surrounded by a boundary fence called a 'park pale' (either a cleft oak fence or a bank surmounted by a cleft oak fence), or by a wall. If there was a bank, then there was normally a ditch on the inside. Park pales often contained 'deer leaps' to entice wild deer into the park (these had a ramp on the outside so deer could enter, and a pit on the inside to prevent them from getting out); this was a source of legal disputes with the Crown, who officially owned all 'wild' deer beyond the pale. Buildings in parks included manor houses (from Tudor times), keepers' lodges, and banqueting houses.

Turf and stone were extracted and mineral coal too, and arable crops might be grown. Some had productive fishponds; a number of these survive today as ornamental features, though others have been abandoned.

CONTESTED LANDSCAPES AND RESOURCES

Woods and other woodland landscapes were hugely valuable resources for local people and we see this in accounts of medieval and later communities in England. All lands and resources in the feudal system were ultimately under the control of the Crown, but rights were gifted, sold, or bartered over time. The net result was potential conflict of interest between, say, a manorial lord and the commoners of the manor. In some cases the system worked smoothly so that each derived what was necessary; in other cases bitter conflicts arose. The issues at stake might include contest for status, and perhaps rights to game such as deer and, at the other end of the spectrum, the access to the resources necessary for survival, such as fuel, building materials, food, and grazing for livestock. Because woods provided so many materials and resources basic to life and survival, sophisticated systems of rights and the supervision of rights evolved. These established customs and traditions were subject to various courts and inquiries in the case of disputes. These might be between commoners, between commoners and the Lord, and between any of these and the Crown estate.

The impact of the feudal system imposed after 1066 included the imposition of Royal Forests and Forest Law, essentially to protect game (especially deer), and timber. This could mean loss of vital resources for local peasant commoners, and conflicts between the Crown, local landowners, and, for example, ecclesiastical estates. Deer were strictly protected but might be gifted to favoured lords or to the church, and they competed with the livestock of commoners and might do serious damage to crops. Furthermore, as iron smelting grew in importance during the late medieval period and into the early industrial times, there were major conflicts between iron masters (wanting timber and wood for charcoal) and local people. The competition extended to shipbuilders who required timber for the navy.

By the eighteenth century and into the nineteenth, enclosures for ornamental parks, of common land for agriculture, and of former open woods for game, led to long-running and often bloody disputes. These were encapsulated in infamous legislation such as the so-called 'Black Act' of 1723, which facilitated the removal of common access to vital resources and turned commoners into poachers to be ruthlessly controlled by gamekeepers.

The law was very lax in terms of controlling or limiting a landowner's right to protect game. This mantrap of the eighteenth or nineteenth century, from Zennor Folk Museum in Cornwall, is a 'good' example of how the commoners were to be kept out of what had often been their common.

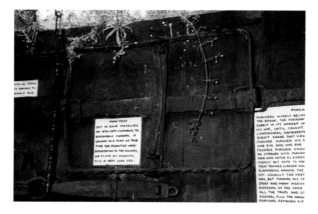

WORKED AND WORKING TREES

CLUES TO PAST WOODLAND uses are the rich resources of once-managed, 'worked', or 'working' trees; what I describe as 'retired veterans'. This heritage is unique to ancient wooded or treed landscapes. Once vital to local and even national interests, the trees were coppiced, pollarded, shredded, stubbed, or grown as maidens for timber. They also produced leaf fodder, bark, coppice wood for fuel and construction, acorns, nuts and mast. Today, long-abandoned, these trees are iconic features rich in biodiversity, their shapes and forms providing unique archives of the past.

Woods and other wooded landscapes were at the heart of pre-industrial society, producing fuel, food and building materials. Essential for transport (such as shipbuilding and the first railway lines), they provided charcoal for heating, cooking, and especially for metal smelting and working. These lands were contested spaces for landowner and peasant over rights and usage, hunting and timber. National security was sometimes at stake, when timber merchants required big trees for shipbuilding but iron masters demanded charcoal for making armour, weapons and cannon. Trees produced pyroligneous acid (wood vinegar: a dark liquid produced through carbonisation if wood is heated and air restricted, as during charcoal production), wood tar and volatile organic compounds (oils and paraffin) for burning and waterproofing, all vital in pre-petrochemical society.

Individual 'worked' trees, if 'ancient', bear the marks of centuries of human exploitation. They might be giant old pollards with massive heavy boughs, or great coppice stools with crowns of re-grown sprouts. These trees have a story to tell of interactions with local people over centuries. Nineteenth-century clergyman and diarist, Reverend Francis Kilvert, gives an impression of these special trees when he describes the ancient oaks of Moccas Park, Herefordshire:

> ... grey, gnarled, low-browed, knock-kneed, bowed, bent, huge, strange, long-armed, deformed, hunchbacked, misshapen, oakmen with both feet in the grave yet tiring down and seeing out generation after generation.

Opposite:
A Victorian print of a woodland and log waggon, showing timbers and large poles being hauled.

Right: Burnham Beeches, London's most famous fuelwood pollards, on a postcard from the early 1900s.

Far right: A selection of rare deadwood beetles: excellent indicators of ancient wood pastures.

Below: The Burnham Beeches pollards and a commoner gathering fallen wood, a print of the 1800s.

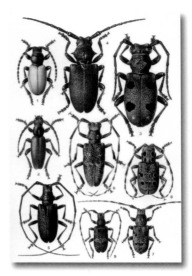

To understand once-worked trees you must appreciate times when woodland and trees were at the centre of local and even national economies. Building required big 'timbers' of the correct size, shape and dimensions, plus smaller 'wood' for in-filling and more modest construction work. The different tree species were selected for their properties: durability, hardness, water- or rot-resistance, flexibility, strength and more.

Great trees might be forced to grow in particular ways and shapes over a hundred or two hundred years to provide materials for ships or buildings. Wood was at the heart of society in ways it is not now, and will never be again.

The consequence of these uses is a remarkable tree heritage, some tall and straight, others bent and

A Woodman's billhook for cutting small wood and trimming off side branches.

Carting logs at an unnamed location. This 1906 postcard shows the heavy horse, a young lad assisting, and the wagon and harness.

Woodland cut stump, showing the results of the woodman's or forester's activities; for oak in particular, the cut stumps may survive a hundred years or more and provide important evidence of the former woodland cover, or of episodes of management.

25

The Oak Parlour at Derwent Hall, Derbyshire (now under the Ladybower Reservoirs), showing the importance of timber in displaying status.

Opposite: The Staple Inn, Holborn, London; an example of a timber building which still exists – possible even in a major city.

bowed, or misshapen tangles of re-growth. Huge pollards of wooded common, forest, or park are instantly recognisable and include many of our most iconic trees. These wonderfully decrepit old giants are so obvious that one might imagine we know where they all are, but we don't. Certainly twenty years ago we didn't, until the Ancient Tree Forum's Big Tree Hunt. This was one of the most popular community-based environmental surveys ever and revolutionised our knowledge and understanding of ancient trees. The work of countless individuals has helped to save old trees that would otherwise have been 'lost'. There is still much to do, and anyone can help by visiting the Ancient Tree Forum website, and surveying their own patch. Our team recently discovered 1,000 to 2,000 previously unrecognised ancient veteran worked trees, in woodland in the heart of the Peak District National Park and close to major cities. Imagine what remains to be found elsewhere, with old veterans still to be found and recorded, in hidden valleys, secret streamsides and ancient hedgerows. Particularly exciting is the recent recognition of massive centuries-old coppice trees. Veteran smaller trees like hawthorn, rowan, birch, holly and hazel provide rich resources for researchers; much older than they appear, as 'worked' trees now retired, they provide insight into the lives and landscapes of the local countryside.

Close-up of an ancient pollard crown in a Suffolk hedgerow, showing the massive re-grown limbs resulting from abandonment.

TYPES OF WORKED TREES

Worked or retired trees provide remarkable insights into wood management, from a few decades ago to centuries past. They fall into two main types: coppice stools (woody re-growths cut back to just above ground level) and pollards, with some less obvious or rather localised types. The more common forms include a raised coppice called a 'stub', which is often found as a significant ancient boundary feature on a woodland edge or old parish boundary. Some coppices, especially from ancient hazels, may mix different ages and sizes of re-growth on one stool (the base of the cut tree), whereas the most common are with all the poles (re-grown shoots) the same age. In upland sites, particularly growing in boulder clutter of rocky scree-slopes, are multi-stemmed 'medusoid' trees, which probably result from coppice use. Some trees like alder and lime coppice naturally by stem growth and fall with age followed by re-growth, or through grazing damage. Some coppice lime trees are around three thousand years old.

Woodland and pollards at Burnham Beeches with sheep grazing in the background.

This ancient coppice stool of small-leaved lime at Whitwell Wood, north Derbyshire, is probably over one thousand years old.

Carting the coppice at Crowborough, east Sussex (postcard from the early 1900s).

WOODLAND CRAFTS
AND OTHER INDUSTRIES

THE PEOPLE involved in managing woods were specialist craftsmen and their families, often undertaking particular crafts for specific markets. Some occurred across the whole of medieval Britain; others were localised or regionally distinctive. They included charcoal burners, white coal makers, clog makers, bodgers, tan-bark merchants, timber merchants, potash makers, basket-makers and others. Alongside woodland crafts were other industries based on particular resources found where woods were located: mining for mineral coal and ironstone, digging building stone, sand and gravel, and quarrying for rock including refractory ganister. All left scars on wooded landscapes.

If we were to step back into a working medieval wood or even an English coppice wood during the 1920s or 1930s, it would hardly be recognisable to our twenty-first-century eyes, noses and ears. These were locally important resources, managed in the same ways, and by the same families, for decades or even centuries. Working woods bustled with life and activity, people and animals working in harmony and varying with the seasons and longer management cycles. Families lived and worked in and around the woods, felling trees, cutting coppice, peeling bark, making besom brooms, constructing hurdle fencing, tending pigs, herding livestock, warrening rabbits, watching over deer, and harvesting nuts. Other workers dug mineral coal and stone, or shallow-mined iron-stone or gravel, depending on where in the country they were and who owned the wood. The woodland workers varied from region to region, for example the 'bodgers' of the Chiltern beech-woods, chair-leg manufacturers supplying part-finished chair-legs cut on pole-lathes from green coppice wood.

Other people worked in and around the coppice wood, including the woodman, cutting timber and wood, perhaps for fuel-wood markets. Cutting wood inside the woodland, and bigger timbers often outside, would be sawyers working in teams: the 'top-dog' standing above and directing the big-handled, two-man saw; the 'underdog' in the pit below. The latter pulled the great saw downwards, probably getting eyefuls of sawdust; it was thirsty work and sawyers were famed beer-drinkers.

Opposite:
Bark peelers at work in the 1930s, stripping the bark from the trunk to supply a local tannery.

Above: An early print of an osier basket-maker manufacturing and selling his wares – this was a practice that occurred almost everywhere in Britain.

Above right: A traditional besom maker or broom squire (1930s) – this was a craft that was prevalent throughout Britain.

Right: Wooden hay-rakes were a typical 'small-wood' product and in great demand in a labour-intensive, traditional rural landscape before mechanisation and de-population.

Hazel coppice-with-standards in the 1930s. Note the open-ground nature of the wood, the limited ground flora, and the tall, straight 'standard' trees for timber at about eighty years.

Making chestnut paling, an important coppice wood product since Roman times.

The woodward oversaw these activities on behalf of the landowner, and from the eighteenth century onwards was joined by gamekeepers and others involved in the rapidly growing industry of game management. Key people were the parker who ran the deer park, and the warrener who dealt more with small game like rabbits and hares. By the nineteenth century, a significant proportion of the working community would be gamekeepers, often employed as hired thugs

33

Above: A wonderful model of a sawpit at Zennor Folk Museum, Cornwall. Note the metal lever to move the great timber over the pit.

Below: A nice selection of traditional pit saws on display at Zennor Folk Museum, Cornwall.

Below right: Sawyers at the pit with the 'topdog' pulling from above, and the unfortunate 'underdog' pulling the two-man saw from below. This was famously hot, dusty work and the sawyers were renowned for drinking copious amounts of beer or ale and for singing along too.

to keep the commoners out of what had once been their woods.

By this time too, with changed society, economy and technology, the numbers of woodland craftsmen were in decline. Many coppice woods ended their last cycle some time between 1800 and 1950 as centuries-old traditions died; since most were oral traditions passed down from generation to generation, as they ended they were lost. Woods, now either changed, or with their function lost were themselves vulnerable to destruction. Therefore, between the beginning of the nineteenth century and the 1980s, huge numbers of ancient woods were abandoned, grubbed up, or re-planted with exotic tree species. Many old coppices that were retained were converted to 'high forests' or modern 'forestry', not to be confused with the ancient 'forests'.

Some people who populated our woodlands past left defining marks still visible in the woods today. This archaeology in contemporary sites can often be tracked back to specific uses and times. In other cases, features are vague and indefinable; some woodland users, for example the tanners who were once almost ubiquitous in woods across the country, left few obvious traces.

Changing fashions in the nineteenth and twentieth centuries are reflected in this image of aristocratic shooters, one of whom is sporting a set of dead foxes.

WOOD, TIMBER AND THE WORK OF THE HOUSEWRIGHT

It was not until the seventeenth century that stone and brick widely supplanted timber and wood as building materials. Timber had held prime place ever since the first permanent settlements built in Neolithic times. Castles and parish churches were constructed of timber before being rebuilt in stone and even then, the core structures were often built around great timbers. Huge numbers of trees from Britain's medieval woods still survive in timber-framed houses and barns. The builder of these, a house carpenter or housewright, unlike his counterpart today, didn't obtain timber as ready-sawn or shaped planks and beams. This master craftsman went to woods (or hedges) and chose trees carefully to match requirements. This timber would, with minimum shaping, roughly square up to the dimensions of the components required: large trees for beams and smaller trees for materials such as rafters. The timber used was usually oak and sometimes elm or sweet chestnut, sawn or shaped with an axe or adze while still 'green' (this made it easier to work). Metal nails

were not used because tannic acid in unseasoned oak quickly corrodes them. Instead, the craftsmen used oak pegs (sometimes called treenails) in their thousands.

England has two traditions of timber-framed building: 'post-and-truss' (or box frame) and 'cruck building'. In most cases, timber-framed buildings were constructed in the house carpenter's yard or 'framing yard', and taken pre-fabricated for on-site assembly. As constructed and originally assembled, every piece of timber for the house or barn was marked to ensure each part was correctly placed when re-erected on its final site. Careful examination of the timbers of an old building may well reveal the marks of the carpenters who built it.

Cruck barn in Herefordshire, showing the main timbers. This was an ancient and traditional north-European style of building construction.

MAKING CHARCOAL AND WHITE COAL

These activities left indelible imprints on the woods. The impact of some industries were more obvious than others; charcoal and 'white coal' are especially significant. Charcoal was widely manufactured but particularly close to iron-smelting sites. In regions such as the English Lake District (supplying the Furness iron works) and north Derbyshire or south Yorkshire (supplying iron and steel factories), the charcoal woods were managed intensively and industrially. This had a massive long-term impact, so while the woods survived because they were economically important, they were changed in character. These activities, in the case of charcoal extending back over two millennia, and for white coal just two to three centuries from the late sixteenth century, left a remarkable heritage. Not only did they change the treescape by coppicing and burning the wood, but they stripped the woods of centuries-old soils and the living fabric of the vegetation too. Turf and sods were cut from the woodland floor to cover the woodmen's wigwam buildings, and to blanket and seal the charcoal burns themselves. Go into one of these woods today and there is no topsoil: just a few centimetres of black charcoal dust and then subsoil. Now, very gradually, fifty to sometimes 150 years after the last charcoal burns, the vegetation slowly

A postcard from 1908, entitled 'A Hearty Meal – Charcoal Burners, Balcombe Forest [Sussex]'. Charcoal burners and other woodland workers were known for their copious eating and drinking.

creeps back. Some plants like bluebells recover quite quickly but others such as wood anemone or the diminutive wood melick grass take much longer.

Charcoal making for iron smelting is often the oldest recorded woodland industry. This is not surprising as, being essential to metal smelting and working, it was used from prehistoric times. Markets for iron-smelting charcoal gradually disappeared during the eighteenth century as mineral coke replaced it. Some demands remained and others expanded. Charcoal was used in

Charcoal burners shown in a Victorian print of Mark Ash Wood, New Forest, Hampshire.

making blister steel in cementation furnaces where successive layers of bar iron inter-bedded with charcoal were heated to high temperatures for up to eight days. Another charcoal-based industry was gunpowder manufacture, using alder, willow, and alder buckthorn. Charcoal was also used in large quantities as blacking by moulders in iron foundries. Away from industrial areas, especially in great halls and houses and before the advent of modern chimneys, charcoal was important for cooking and heating. It burns predictably hot and clean. Wood fuel is variable and messy, and coal produces unpleasant and even dangerous fumes; in open or primitive fireplaces, neither is ideal for cooking. High-quality charcoal was needed for gas masks, for medicinal use, and by artists.

During the 'coaling' season, generally from April to November, charcoal burners or 'wood colliers' lived isolated lives, often with their families, deep in the woodlands. Their work consisted of burning carefully stacked lengths of coppice poles in the absence of enough air for complete combustion. During this controlled burning, moisture was driven off, followed by volatile elements of tar and creosote. The process left behind residual black carbon with a little ash. Everything was saved; the ashes were used as covering for subsequent burns.

Charcoal-burners on site in England in the early 1900s, showing the whole family at work raking, sieving, and watching – even the dog is involved. Note the charcoal product carefully stacked in sacks.

Charcoal-burners' hut, Markash, New Forest (1920s); note the turf roof.

Using traditional methods but with subtle variations in layout, a level spot was chosen and the turf removed. This was about 15 feet in diameter and called the pitstead, pit, or hearth. On a steep site, the platform was dug out from the hillside. The stack was built and the wood was then covered by straw, grass, bracken, and turves, which in turn were covered by dust and ashes. Virtually all air was excluded and the burn could be controlled.

Charcoal-burners' hut, Gillwell Park, from a postcard published by J. Farringdon (1930s–40s). This may have been a mock-up rather than a working hut.

Red-hot charcoal and a few dry sticks were dropped down the central flue. When the stack was alight, the wood collier sealed the flue, and fire spread through the stack. It was important the burn was steady and fire did not break through to the surface allowing air in. The burner had to be in constant attendance during the burn, with hurdle fencing and sacking to protect his stack from sudden wind changes; closing gaps in the stack with bracken, turf, and soil. Burning lasted anything from two to ten days depending on stack size, weather conditions, and wood greenness. The burn emitted clouds of white smoke, gradually turning blue and then dying away altogether, each stage indicating how the burn progressed. When the firing was over, the stack was uncovered with a rake to cool and the charcoal, a valuable product but liable to fragmentation, was carefully packed into sacks or panniers for transportation.

The same charcoal hearths and the charcoal makers' hut sites were reused repeatedly at the end of each coppice cycle for a particular area of woodland. As shown in photographs, the huts were conical in shape, built on a framework of poles like a wigwam around a low perimeter stone wall. This is one of the oldest and most primitive forms of building known to humanity and its survival to the twentieth century in cities like Sheffield is quite remarkable. The remains of these huts in the form of a circle of stones (the remains of the low perimeter wall with a gap for the doorway), can still be found in some parts of England (north and west). Each particular craftsman, be it a wood collier, clog maker, or bark stripper, had their own distinctive type of hut – each related and similar but different and distinctive.

Charcoal-burning in the Lake District, from a series published by James Atkinson in 1904. The burn has finished and the hard work of sorting and sieving has begun.

Alongside charcoal making was another woodland industry: making fuel for metal-smelting in woods in north Wales, southern Scotland, the Yorkshire Dales, south Yorkshire, and north Derbyshire. This was more localised than charcoal manufacture and was associated with lead smelting. Lead ore was smelted with a mix of this dried wood called 'white coal' or 'chop-wood'. In south Yorkshire, the lead was carried from Derbyshire, from the relatively poorly wooded Peak District to water-powered ore-hearths located on the fast-flowing rivers near the region's coppice woods. White coal was small lengths of wood, dried in a kiln until all the moisture was driven out. Charcoal and white coal were mixed together to smelt lead, because charcoal gave too high a temperature and wood not high enough, or white coal was used alone in smelting lead ore with charcoal used to re-smelt the slag.

Characteristic large depressions or craters in the wood confirm the former presence of white-coal production in a wood. These can be anything from 3 to 5 metres in diameter with a noticeable 'flue' at one end. The flues face downhill, varying in length and construction. These are the remains

Charcoal-burner covering the stack. The skills of constructing and covering the stack of wood to be 'burnt' were among the trade secrets of the coleman or collier.

of white coal kilns, sometimes also known as 'Q-pits' (because the letter 'Q' mirrors the shape of the archaeological remains). In Sheffield, there remains a persistent rumour or myth, that these are bomb craters from German bombers that targeted the city during the Second World War.

OAK-BARK LEATHER TANNING

Other woodland workers included tanners and bark peelers who stripped the bark off timber and coppice wood (giving rise to the surnames Tanner and Barker). The bark was vital, alongside faeces, for manufacturing leather, again essential in pre-petrochemical society. The bark peelers were separate from the charcoal burners and this can be recognised in the differing shapes and styles of their temporary buildings now reduced to archaeological remains; each is distinctive. Bark peeling for tanning was of such national importance that in 1603 there was passed 'An Act concerning Tanners, Curriers, Shoemakers and other Artificers occupying the cutting of Leather'. This act stated that '... for as much as barke is of late become verie dear and skarce, which happeneth partlie by reason that divers persons do ingrosse & buy great quantities thereof', and goes on to explain in detail the regulations and controls over cutting, peeling and selling bark. The Act was not repealed until 1808.

Opposite:
Felling the tree to peel the bark, 1930s.

Loading the bark to cart it to the tannery, 1930s. Like all woodland products the material had to be transported off site – sometimes as a finished or part-finished product, or in the case of tanbark, to be processed and used elsewhere.

Just as salt and wood were hugely important in medieval societies, tanned leather was a massively valuable and essential product. Christine Handley has researched the history of wood-bark tanning, discovering that during the 150-year period from 1680 to 1830, the production of leather and leather goods was, by value, the second most important industry in England after textiles. The leather industry was one of the largest employers outside agriculture. Woodlands played a major role in supplying tree-bark, which before the introduction of chemical substitutes, was the main agent, in the form of a liquor, used in the preparation or 'tanning' of the animal hides. This was prior to their conversion into such everyday articles as boots, shoes, clogs, harnesses, saddles, breeches, aprons, gloves, bags, cases and bottles, and for use in industry for bellows and belting. Bookbinders were also important customers for fine leather. The tannic acid from ground bark seeps slowly through the pores of the hide, draws out the water, and coats each fibre with a preservative. The tannin content of oak-bark made it the most efficient and therefore the most important tanning agent.

When a woodland compartment was coppiced the wood might first be de-barked. The bark was peeled in large pieces from both the timber trees and the underwood poles. This was done by scoring a tree around its trunk

Bark peelers at work in the 1930s – the tree lies naked, stripped of its bark.

at 2-foot intervals, and making a longitudinal slit along the trunk. The bark was levered off in large plates with a bark peeler called a 'spud'. It was often the practice to remove as much bark as possible while the tree was standing, then felling it to strip the rest. The peeled bark was stacked to dry. As tannin is soluble in water, it was protected from rain in thatched stacks until sold to tanners. The woodland historian and archaeologist should also be on the lookout for the remains of tanneries in well-wooded areas, which contained bark-mills worked with horse or waterpower. Here the bark was ground into tan-pits, through which the hides were successively passed. These tan-pits contained increasingly strong tannin solutions. Today, there are very few tanneries in England still using oak tannins for leather production.

POTASH MANUFACTURE

Alkali made from the ash of green plant material was hugely important to the textile industry and was used in various dyeing processes. Potash, as it was known, was also used with other ashes for domestic soap, and was an important fertiliser. Until recently, the process of potash making was unclear, but we now know it involved two stages, which left very different evidence. There were massive stone-built kilns, open at the top and bottom, for

Another ubiquitous activity undertaken using bark from the wood, but on an industrial or at least commercial basis, was the tanning of leather, as shown in this 1930s photograph. The bark released tannins into a mix of chemicals which included urine, animal faeces and decaying flesh, making ancient tanneries particularly smelly.

burning leaves and other green vegetation. This produced base-rich ash, which was taken and boiled in large metal cauldrons seated in pits cut into earthen banks. To produce caustic potash, the mix was heated on a metal plate over a hot fire. Potash and ashes mixed with animal fat or tallow were used for soap manufacture. Evidence can be seen in variable and often shallow depressions and pits, which may have been where the 'elying' took place or could be the sites of less industrial ash burning. Potash makers probably operated quite widely but are only known of in detail from Cumbria. Here the process was undertaken on an industrial scale to supply Lancashire's textile manufacturing.

THE SMALL CRAFTS

In pre-petrochemical society, natural products such as wood were hugely important for making items such as the wood-turned bowls shown here.

Less well-known but once widespread are a number of specialist, often outdoor woodland crafts, which have now almost disappeared. This is because either the product is no longer required and other materials are used, or the products are now made in factories. Such crafts include turnery, coopering, chair bodging and the manufacture of wheels, clogs, baskets, hurdles, thatch spars, rakes, besoms, hazel hoops (to put around barrels), and brush handles. At least a further dozen or so crafts could be added to the list.

Turners made not only wooden dishes and plates but also a wide range of kitchen and dairy implements, and until the 1970s, they made wooden clothes pegs and clothes-wringer rollers. Today's wood turners are more likely to be making decorative objects and toys. Like turners, coopers also made vessels for food: 'dry coopers' made casks to hold non-liquid goods; 'white coopers' made articles for domestic use; and 'wet coopers' produced casks for storing liquids. The wet cooper made a whole range of specialised vessels including pails and piggins for carrying water and milk, churns for making butter, tubs called keelers for cooling liquids, tubs called kimnels for general use, lidded kits for holding milk, and hogsheads for storing ale.

Clog-makers used alder, willow, birch, sycamore and beech trees. Alder was preferred because it was waterproof and easy to work. Short lengths of tree trunk were riven (split) into sole blocks by the clog-sole maker and shaped with a special tool called a stock knife.

Besom making was also a widespread local craft until the beginning of the twentieth century. Besoms were indispensable for sweeping flagged cottage floors and factory floors. The besom handles were made from young ash, birch or hazel poles and the brooms from bundles of birch or hazel twigs, or from heather or broom. These were tied together originally with strips of willow, riven oak, or even bramble.

Wood-turned products such as these chair legs were produced on site in vast quantities by 'bodgers'. The practice was especially important in the Chilterns, where the legs were part-finished on site to be transported off site for completion. A 'bodged' job is not necessarily bad: it is just part done.

A besom maker at work binding a head of young twigs, probably birch; heather was also used.

Basket-making was also a widespread craft with great regional variation in the type of basket made, from swill baskets made of thin strips of boiled oak to fish 'kiddles', made of willow and used for trapping fish.

Many crafts occurred widely but varied in time and intensity. Some industries, such as potash manufacture in south Cumbria, chair-leg bodging in the Chilterns and white-coal production in or near lead mining areas, were important regional specialisms. The regional and local variations are reflected in documentary records and in the archaeology of local woods.

A traditional spelk basket maker using thin slivers of split wood. This is a swill or oak spelk basket and a traditional product of northern England. The raw material was oak poles bought from a local bark peeler (and so without bark). This was then riven, boiled, split, and peeled into layers, which were then woven into a basket.

MINERAL AND STONE EXTRACTION

Other industrial remains occur alongside industrial processes which used woodland resources directly. Examples of these other industries include glass-making, smelting, metal working, quarrying and brick-making, found extensively in woods and on wooded heaths.

Since the Neolithic flint miners of Norfolk's Brecklands, people have quarried, mined and dug for minerals and stone. Sometimes these sites were in wooded landscapes, and in other cases, following abandonment of the post-minerals sites the woodland re-established to cover the wounds of industrial activity. Either way our woods are often pockmarked with anything from small stone-getting pits for local wall building, to major bell-pits for mineral coal or ironstone, to extensive survey cutting of coal and large quarries for ganister or limestone. Others sites have large gravel pits, clay sites and sandpits. Many small stone-getting or other pits and features are not easily defined or classified and just have to be accepted as an intriguing part of the wood's long history.

The woodman used a variety of specialist and generalist tools – such as this adze or mattock.

WOODLAND ARCHAEOLOGY AND ECOLOGY

ANCIENT WOODLAND can provide a living record of past woodland management practices and the organisation of the landscape. The traces left by the woodland crafts and the workers and families include where they lived, the worked trees (old pollards and coppice stools, for example), platforms, processing areas and trackways. These represent the archaeology *of* the woods, and along with internal and external wood banks, ditches, walls and other evidence, are closely tied to the history of the wood and its existence through history. Other people living and working in woods, such as quarrymen and miners, also left evidence, such as remnant charcoal pits, ore furnaces and kilns. This is the archaeology *in* the woods but not *of* the woods. In many sites, this is a huge part of the modern-day landscape and tells unique stories of human interaction with environmental resources. The story runs from prehistoric times, to the medieval and early industrial, right up to the present day. Throughout history, all the people using the woods, and living in and around them, left their mark.

The changes in land use can be identified in the various internal and external boundary features; so a medieval deer park may have large external banks and even walls, plus an internal ditch to keep the deer in. There might be earthworks within the wood that are the remains of deer management features. Converted from a park to a coppice wood the site may have internal banks and ditches to mark out the different coppice compartments, and a ditch outside the boundary bank in order to keep grazing animals out. In some regions such as north Derbyshire or south Yorkshire, traditional medieval coppices were replaced by intensive industrial coppice for iron and steel industries, again leaving distinctive evidence. For many sites, the nineteenth and twentieth centuries saw traditions abandoned and replacement by exotic 'high forest' of non-native tree species like European larch, Norway spruce, and Scots pine (not native outside the Highlands). Sycamore and beech were widely used. Many woods were converted to conifer or sycamore plantations. Others in urban areas

Opposite:
A Victorian print of a woodland pond – with people and working animals in the woods, and often living and working there, ponds and other features would have been commonplace to supply essential water.

High coppice of stubs dating from the 1980s miners' strike in Barnsley – a distinctive form of coppice formed as the miners scavenged for fuelwood and cut the trees from a kneeling position as they would hew coal underground. This has produced a unique coalminer's high coppice dating solely from this time.

became amenity woods, often with clinically tidy management and emphasis on access provision often at the expense of conservation.

LOOKING FOR THE INDICATORS

Romano-British enclosure photographed in Scholes Coppice, Rotherham in 1959 – an example of archaeology 'in' a wood.

Ancient woods have antiquity and continuity of woodland cover, providing refuge over centuries for a great variety of plants and animals, even while

Outgrown coppice, perhaps eighty years old on a two-hundred-year-old stool, at Wortley (near Sheffield) in about 1900.

Herb Paris is an excellent but very rare indicator of ancient woods – today only usually found on base-rich soils.

the surrounding landscapes have seen major changes. Consequently, ancient woods are often very rich in wildlife, and have undisturbed soil profiles and natural water features.

Wooded environments provide ideal conditions for special plants and animals that

The common dog violet is an indicator plant often found in ancient woods.

are often only found in woods and wooded landscapes. Some of these are good 'indicators' of ancient woodlands and can be used to help find, identify, and verify our ancient woods. Reading the landscape mixes archaeological humps and bumps with identification of woodland plants and animals. Helpfully for the beginner, many of the woodland wildflowers are familiar, easy to identify, and along with trees, can be read like a book – as long as you know the language. These indicators, along with soils, can be a rich source of information on history and former management. Bear in mind that both the presence and the unexpected absence of key species can provide clues to the past.

SOME INDICATOR SPECIES AND WHAT THEY TELL US

Indicator species can include flowering plants especially but also many groups of animals, particularly insects. The latter, however, are really for the specialist and here we are interested in the 'easy to use' wild flowers. These indicators include familiar plants like the wild bluebell and the white-flowered greater stitchwort. An indicator flower can draw attention to a wood being maybe old or even ancient, or perhaps a fragment of a wood now long-since lost. Indicators are generally reliable because they have an ecological attachment to very old woodland and in most cases, they don't easily spread to new sites. Indicator flowers are affected by soils and geology – so whether the site is on limestone or chalk, or on sandstone,

Massed wood anemone is an excellent indicator of old woodland.

for example, can make a big difference. On limey soils many indicators spread far more easily; particularly in the warmer, more humid conditions of the west coast. In the drier east and south-east they are more tightly confined to old woods.

Woodland indicators help to find a 'wood' but they also score towards the site being ancient, and essentially the more of these species found, the more likely it is that the wood is old. There are thirty to forty flowers which we include as 'indicators', and if the number found at a site reaches double figures then it is time to be excited. Some plants are only slightly associated with a wood being old, but others, like wood anemone and yellow archangel, are generally strong indicators. These plants can also be clues to past management: common cow-wheat is associated with former coppice sites, for example. The diminutive wood sorrel can cling on in remote upland sites as an indicator perhaps of former woodland cover. Coppice trees and shrubs can suggest former use such as charcoal manufacture, and shrubs

Red campion,
a wild flower of
woodland edge
and hedgerow but
not necessarily
indicative of
ancient woods.

Wood sorrel, an indicator of ancient woods and relicts, often found in upland areas.

Wild garlic, an indicator of damp ancient woods.

such as alder buckthorn may have been introduced specifically for making fine-quality charcoal for gunpowder. Even exotic plants can help tell a story of the woodland's past, with the common rhododendron, snowberry, and other shrubs often introduced for Victorian game shooting. Exotic conifers like European larch and various pines may relate to the abandonment of traditional coppice and the development in the eighteenth and nineteenth centuries of so-called 'high forest'. Within the wood, certain plants, such as the hairy woodrush, may be ancient woodland indicators but associated with sites of small-scale disturbance. The pretty and distinctive grass wood melick is strongly associated with the woodland edge – wood banks and the deep sides of medieval hollow-ways. The distribution of woodland flowers is influenced strongly by topography, soils, and moisture within the wood. So bluebell carpets drier ground, often with honeysuckle, and wild garlic favours damp soils and sheltered, streamside valley-bottoms.

THE FUTURE: RE-DISCOVERING THE OLD CRAFTS

MANY WOODLAND CRAFTS, having survived as oral traditions down the centuries, succumbed quickly to urbanisation and industrialisation during the early twentieth century. Of some of these, we know very little. However, in other cases such as charcoal making, the skills were rescued and recorded from the very brink of oblivion, often in the 1950s. In this way the old skills and traditions were demonstrated, recorded, and passed on. Some crafts were written about in estate records and aspects of use can be elucidated from the archives. Mel Jones' archival research in south Yorkshire, for example, has given a fascinating insight into the precise and particular management of sites and trees. This can be down to the exact day on which trees were cut and used, the people involved in both buying and selling, and the actual price paid. Some crafts and their products remain shrouded in mystery, and even if records were made and survive, they often use words

Contemporary wood crafts at Eyam, north Derbyshire.

A 1990s
re-construction
and revival
charcoal burn at
Whitwell Wood,
North Derbyshire.

to describe materials and amounts that are obscure and difficult for us to decipher. These are lost crafts and skills that will never be recreated and for which even their products are long-since obsolete.

Today there is a growing interest in rediscovering the old uses and the old ways. Only a few people actually make a living since the work is hard, and often requires attention on-site twenty-four hours a day, seven days a week. This is the case when a charcoal burn is on. Aside from the satisfaction of traditions maintained and jobs well done, the rewards are scant. New craftsmen make

Postcard showing
a modern craft
woodworker.

Postcard showing a modern osier basket-maker.

a living from the craft and education, selling both product and process. As old crafts and skills died away, woods have survived, just. As described earlier, many sites were converted into conifer plantations, or ploughed up between 1940 and 1980. The remaining woods hold a unique archive, the footprints and ghosts of the men, women and families who lived and worked the woods for centuries. There are moves today to re-discover old woods and remove the imposed conifers or sycamores. In a few cases, there are attempts to put the craftsman or -woman back into the woods as well. Yet this can only be a token gesture since the work is hard and poorly paid, and for now at least, we simply don't depend on the working woods as we once did. However, there is a new breed of woodland craft workers who harvest timber and work with grain — the wood carvers. These people can help to build a bridge to the woodland crafts of the past, and it can be rewarding both spiritually and financially. This is a new forward-thinking approach, which can join green wood turners, charcoal-burners, hurdle makers, clog makers, local people and conservation managers in growing a new awareness and attachment to their local woods.

CONSERVATION

In the twenty-first century, all is not as well as it might seem in Britain's woods. On the one hand, the woods have regenerated and are rejuvenated by abandonment and so tall trees grow where once there was a scrubby coppice. However, as the high canopy or the outgrown coppice becomes dense, the light is closed out and the glorious mats of woodland ground flora, the bluebells, anemones and wild garlic, disappear. Furthermore, as governmental planners and others turn their eyes to bio-fuels from

Ancient woodland re-planted as high forest conifers.

the woods, a use that they argue is in keeping with their origins, an even worse and more damaging fate awaits them. Instead of manpower, horses and oxen to work the modern woods, these contemporary industrialists apply a single man on a huge tracked vehicle, which can extract and process large timber all at once. Such industrial and mechanised extraction should not be allowed in 'ancient woods'. Generally when this type of use occurs there has been no meaningful survey of the woodland landscape and certainly not of veteran worked trees. The tracked vehicles used, so-called 'low-impact' machines, can have a devastating effect on the ground, erasing an ancient landscape and its banks, ditches, pits and platforms in just a few hours. I liken this to taking a felt-pen to scribble over the oil paint of the Mona Lisa: you still have a picture but it is not what it was.

Currently, aside from a few dedicated local and regional groups across Britain, very few woodlands have been surveyed for their heritage interest; there is much to be done. In order to safeguard this unique heritage – a living landscape – it needs to be found, recognised and cared for.

Modern damage and threats: forestry vehicle tracks through a scheduled monument in publicly owned ancient woodland in north Derbyshire. The comment from the Forestry Commission national advisor was that these woods have to 'earn their keep'.

FURTHER READING

Three key references to follow up the information given in this book are:

Jones, M. *Sheffield's Woodland Heritage*, 4th edition. Wildtrack Publishing, 2009.

Rotherham, I. D., Jones, M., Smith, L. and Handley, C. (eds.)
The Woodland Heritage Manual: A Guide to Investigating Wooded Landscapes.
Wildtrack Publishing, 2008.

Rotherham, I. D. *Reading the Woodland Landscape*. Wildtrack Publishing, 2013.

To support these texts, information can be downloaded from www.ukeconet.co.uk. There is a series of short leaflets (select 'Community Projects', then 'Discovering Neighbourhood Woodlands') designed specifically to help the beginner in their woodland survey and alongside these are custom-made survey forms and sheets to complete.

- Surveying a Woodland
- An Introduction to Documentary Research
- History, Structure and Form
- Pits, Platforms, Banks and Ditches
- Botanical Indicators
- Worked Trees

For the ecology and trees, some basic field guides to wildflowers and to tree identification are needed. Most woodlands have a specific and quite limited range of flowers and these are generally rather distinctive, so they are fairly easy to survey. The woodland grasses are important indicators too, and though many people find them intimidating to identify, with a little practice, or perhaps guided by a friendly local botanist, the ten or so species you need to recognise will be mastered.

Also relevant are the websites of the Woodland Trust
(www.woodlandtrust.org.uk) and the Ancient Tree Forum
(www.ancient-tree-forum.org.uk).

There is a rich body of literature on woods and their heritage, including
the following, which are highly recommended:

Fowler, J. *Landscapes and Lives: The Scottish Forest through the Ages*.
Canongate Books, 2002.

Hayman, R. *Trees, Woodlands and Western Civilization*. Hambledon &
London, 2003.

Marren, P. *Woodland Heritage*. David & Charles, 1990.

Marren, P. *The Wild Woods*. David & Charles, 1992.

Muir, R. *Ancient Trees: Living Landscapes*. Tempus Publishing Ltd, 2005.

Perlin, J. *A Forest Journey*. Harvard University Press, 1989.

Peterken, G. F. *Woodland Conservation and Management*. Chapman & Hall, 1981.

Peterken, G. F. *Natural Woodland: Ecology and conservation in northern temperate regions*. Cambridge University Press, 1996.

Rackham, O. *Trees and Woodland in the British Landscape*. Dent, 1976 (updated and reprinted 1992).

Rackham, O. *Ancient Woodland: Its history, vegetation and uses in England*. Edward Arnold, 1980 (new, updated edition by Castlepoint Press, 2003).

Rackham, O. *The History of the Countryside*. Dent, 1986.

Rackham, O. *Woodlands*. Collins, 2006.

Rotherham, I. D. (ed.) *The History, Ecology and Archaeology of Medieval Parks and Parklands*. Wildtrack Publishing, 2007.

Smout, T. C., MacDonald, A. R. and Watson, F. *A History of the Native Woodlands of Scotland, 1500–1920*. Edinburgh University Press, 2005.

Vera, F. *Grazing Ecology and Forest History*, CABI Publishing, 2000.

Watkins, C. *Woodland Management and Conservation*. David & Charles, 1990.

PLACES TO VISIT

For information on your local woods visit the Woodland Trust website or contact your local Woodland Trust group or officer or your local tree wardens. Each county also has a Wildlife Trust and many of their nature reserves include ancient woodlands. The Forestry Commission and National Trust may also have regional offices to provide information about forest parks, trails and woods, and often own and manage parks and woods open to the public. Very often, your local authority will have tree and woodland officers, and countryside services. Especially useful are the many community forests around the country and these often have leaflets and guides to local sites and information on their websites.

The information below is just a taster selection of the sort of information that is readily available.

NATIONAL

Woodland Trust Visit Woods website with location and travel information: http://visitwoods.org.uk/en/visit-woods — easy-access, user-friendly information for the whole of the UK and Northern Ireland.

Woodland Trust: www.allaboutyou.com/country/day-out/ 25-wonderfulwoodlands-to-visit-56397

The National Trust cares for a number of woodlands throughout the country and details can be found on their website: www.nationaltrust.org.uk

Ancient Woodland Days: www.wild-things.org.uk/woodlanddays.html

The Wildlife Trusts: www.wildlifetrusts.org has links to county trust sites.

REGIONAL

The New Forest Visitor Centre: www.newforestnpa.gov.uk/visiting/
new-forest-centre

North York Moors National Park: www.northyorkmoors.org.uk/
ancient-woodland

Lincolnshire Lime Woods: http://microsites.lincolnshire.gov.uk/Limewoods

The Chilterns Woodlands: www.chilternsaonb.org/about-
chilterns/woodlands

Cheshire Wildlife Trust has a number of reserves, such as Brookheys Covert:
www.cheshire01.shared.hosting.zen.co.uk/res_brookheys

Forestry Commission: South Yorkshire Community Woodlands:
www.forestry.gov.uk/southyorkshire

The Heritage Woodlands of the South Yorkshire Forest:
www.heritagewoodsonline.co.uk/wood

Surrey County Council, Woodlands: www.surreycc.gov.uk/environment-
housing-and-planning/countryside/woodlands/living-
woodlands/living-woodlands-sites

Sheffield City Council: www.sheffield.gov.uk/out--about/parks-woodlands--
countryside/trees--woodlands.html

INDIVIDUAL LOCAL WOODS & FORESTS

Blean Ancient Woodlands, Blean, Canterbury, CT2 9LD: www.theblean.co.uk

Cotterill Clough: www.cheshire01.shared.hosting.zen.co.uk/res_cotterill

Limekiln Wood, Owley Wood or Warburton's Wood:
www.cheshire01.shared.hosting.zen.co.uk/res_warburtons

Hill Holt Wood: http://hillholtwood.com

Ecclesall Woods, Sheffield: www.friendsofecclesallwoods.org.uk

The Ancient Woods of the Gleadless Valley, Sheffield: www.heritagewoods
online.co.uk/map/026/Gleadless%20Valley%20Pamphlet.pdf

Roundball Wood, Honiton, Devon: www.honiton.gov.uk/Core/Honiton-
Town-Council/UserFiles/Files/RoundballWood/Roundballleaflet.pdf

Epping Forest: www.cityoflondon.gov.uk/things-to-do/green-
spaces/epping-forest

Burnham Beeches and *Stoke Common*: www.cityoflondon.gov.uk/things-to-
do/green-spaces/burnham-beeches-and-stoke-common

Forest of Dean: www.forestry.gov.uk/forestofdean

Sherwood Forest: www.sherwoodforest.org.uk

Bradfield Woods, National Nature Reserve, Suffolk: www.suffolkwildlife
trust.org/reserves-and-visitor-centres/bradfield-woods

Wytham Woods, Oxfordshire: www.wildcru.org/wytham/access.php

Hatfield Forest, Essex: www.nationaltrust.org.uk/hatfield-forest

INDEX

Page numbers in italics refer to illustrations